School Bus ®

KICKS UP A STORM

A BOOK ABOUT WEATHER

SCHOLASTIC INC.
New York   Toronto   London   Auckland   Sydney
Mexico City   New Delhi   Hong Kong   Buenos Aires

From an episode of the animated TV series
produced by Scholastic Entertainment Inc.
Based on *The Magic School Bus* books
written by Joanna Cole and illustrated by Bruce Degen.

TV tie-in book adaptation by Nancy White and illustrated by Art Ruiz.
TV script written by John May, Brian Meehl, and Jocelyn Stevenson.

ISBN-13: 978-0-439-10275-9
ISBN-10: 0-439-10275-8

12 11 10 9 8 7 6 5 4   8 9 10 11 12/0

Printed in the U.S.A.   23

Let me tell you about the day Ralphie decided he was a superhero. It started one hot morning when we were sitting around the classroom. I mean, it was really hot. There wasn't a breath of air. It was the kind of day that gives new meaning to the words "When you're hot, you're hot."

In spite of the heat, Carlos was working on his science project. Then — enter the Friz! (That's what we sometimes call our teacher, Ms. Frizzle.) She was wearing an amazing outfit, even for her. And she was singing!

"I know what we need to clear up this muggy weather," said Ralphie, looking out the window. "A big thunderstorm."

"You mean with thunder and . . . and lightning?" asked Arnold. It was only nine o'clock and already Arnold was beginning to think this was one of those days he should have stayed home.

The idea of a thunderstorm was giving Ralphie a brainstorm. "What if I could *make* a thunderstorm? It would be Ralphie to the rescue!"

I *like* sweating. I hear it's good for you!

"I wouldn't even be Ralphie anymore," Ralphie said to himself.
"I'd be WEATHERMAN!"
And that's how this all started.

In the next instant, Ms. Frizzle brought Ralphie back to the real world.

"How would you like to join our discussion about weather, Ralphie?" she asked.

"Sure," said Ralphie. "Weather is my specialty. Weather is how all the air above and around us is right now."

Weatherman is my name, weather is my game!

Yeah, right.

"No it's not," Carlos objected. "It's water that makes the weather. You know, water, as in RAIN?"

Then Dorothy Ann chimed in. "According to my research, it's air that makes the weather. Moving air, as in WIND."

Keesha disagreed . . . naturally. "Let's get this straight — heat makes the weather, as in HEAT FROM THE SUN!"

Ms. Frizzle said everyone was right. "Air, water, and heat stirred together make weather," she explained.

Then the Friz announced that we were going on — you guessed it — a field trip! Carlos set up his rain catcher outside, just in case it rained while we were gone.

We couldn't believe our eyes when we saw our bus. It looked like a weird weather machine.

Ralphie was back to his Weatherman thing. Before we got on the bus, he announced, "I, Weatherman, will show you how to make weather. I will even make a thunderstorm! But first, we shall explore one of weather's major ingredients — AIR!"

"Excuse me?" said Keesha. "What's to explore? Air is all over the place."

"Do you think I mean just plain old sitting-around air? I'm talking about *moving air*!" said Ralphie.

Then we all got on the bus.

We couldn't believe that Ms. Frizzle actually let Ralphie take over the controls. Maybe the heat was getting to her brain, too. Ralphie pressed a button, pulled some levers, and the giant fan behind the bus turned on.

The next thing we knew, the bus was rising up in the air, and the top was opening up.

And the *next* thing we knew, we all changed into super-light versions of ourselves. We were floating out the top and into the air.

"Look at that humongous cloud," said Carlos. "Too bad it's not over my rain catcher."

"And look how sunny it is over there," said Tim.

"According to my research," said Dorothy Ann, "weather is different in different places. That's because various combinations of wind, water, and heat make many kinds of weather." D.A. really is smart, I have to admit.

When we looked back at the bus, it had sprouted wings and turned into a glider. Our bus does stuff like that.

Look, Ma, no ground!

I knew I should have stayed home todaaaaaaayyyyy!!!

We never did this in my old school!

Listen, you guys. All Ralphie did was turn on a giant fan!

"The world isn't really filled with big fans," said Wanda when we were all back on the bus. "So what really makes the wind?"

"I'll answer that," said Keesha, "but then Ralphie has to make a thunderstorm."

What really makes wind is a combination of air and heat.

The sun heats the earth. Warm earth heats the air closest to it. The heated air rises because warm air is lighter than cool air.

When the warm air rises, more air has to take its place, so cool air rushes in.

And this air movement creates wind.

"Okay, one thunderstorm coming up," promised Ralphie, back at the controls. "I'll just crank up the wind . . . add some heat . . . more heat . . . more wind . . . more heat . . . more . . . oops!"

The bus started spiraling up and up and up. Any normal teacher would have been worried, but not the Friz. She was all excited that Ralphie had created an updraft. She explained that an updraft is warm air that blows up instead of sideways. It's sort of like heat waves coming out of a toaster, only much, much, much bigger.

After Ralphie mixed air and heat to make an updraft, some of the kids
actually started calling him Weatherman. Keesha couldn't believe it.

"How about clouds?" asked Wanda. "Can you make clouds, too,
Weatherman?"

"Why certainly, Wanda," said Ralphie. "I'll just, er . . ."

"You need water," piped up Phoebe. "Clouds are made out of water. I learned
that in my old school."

Then Ralphie pulled another lever, and without so much as a "Shikka-shikka-KABOOM," we turned into water! You could see right through us. Carlos even put his arm right through Arnold!

This is ridiculous!

The bus started changing, too. It turned into a giant seltzer bottle and sprayed us out into the air! If we had been real water, the sun would have warmed us and made us evaporate into the air. But this was much more fun.

"Weatherman has turned us from water into tiny droplets," Ms. Frizzle explained. (Now she was calling Ralphie "Weatherman," too!) "Keep together, class!"

"We are making a cloud!" shouted Wanda.

"Thanks to me, Weatherman!" yelled Weatherman . . . I mean Ralphie.

"It's cold up here," Arnold complained. "I knew I should have brought a sweater."

"The air is so cold way up here, we're turning into ice crystals," Ms. Frizzle told us.

"We're also falling," observed Carlos. And sure enough, he was right.

Ms. Frizzle explained that when ice crystals in a cloud grow and stick together, they get heavy and fall.

"Look on the bright side," said D.A. "The lower we fall, the warmer we get."

"Which must be why we're melting!" yelled Tim.

Ralphie was really on a power trip now. "Weatherman made rain!" he shouted.

Luckily, our bus didn't fail us. It had turned back into a glider, but now it had a giant funnel on top. We rained into the funnel and right back into the bus. We were kids again!

Everyone thought it had been neat being a cloud, then ice crystals, and then falling down as rain. But Keesha was still not impressed.

"Okay, *RALPHIE*," she said (being sure to call him Ralphie and not Weatherman), "so you made a little cloud and a little rain. But where's the thunderstorm?"

"Weatherman will not disappoint you!" promised Ralphie. He was at the controls again. "Make an updraft!" he shouted as he pulled some levers. "Make a cloud! Freeze the water!"

More heat! More water! More wind! Shikka-shikka-KABOOM!!!

The wind roared. Rain poured down. Thunder boomed. Lightning flashed. Weatherman had really made a thunderstorm . . . and we were right inside it!

"Look," said Carlos in amazement, "it's raining UP!"

"That's right, Carlos," said Ms. Frizzle. "Moist air in the rising updraft cools, and condenses into clouds. If the air gets cold enough, the moisture turns to ice crystals, then snow. When the snow gets heavy enough, it falls. As it gets warmer, it turns to rain."

Poor Ralphie was starting to look a little sick. "This is too much," he wailed. "I've got to make it stop!"

"Sorry, Weatherman," said Ms. Frizzle, "but a storm like this won't stop until it's all rained out."

"Listen, I'm not really Weatherman." Ralphie sounded desperate. "I'm just Ralphie. I didn't know what I was doing. I was just pulling levers to show off!"

The bus shrinks. . . .
Weatherman thinks.

The moment Ralphie pulled that last lever, the bus shrank to the size of a Ping-Pong ball. We were all tiny. The raindrops outside looked HUGE.

"Oh, no," Ralphie groaned, "I pulled the shrinker-scope! Now I've made things even worse."

I guess Keesha felt sorry for Ralphie, because she started being a lot nicer to him. "Come on, Weatherman," she said. "You can get us out of this. Just think!"

Ralphie brightened right up when he heard Keesha call him Weatherman.

As Ralphie thought, the tiny bus got caught in an updraft and started going up higher in the air. It was colder up there, so now there were huge snowflakes instead of huge raindrops. Ralphie started muttering to himself.

"Let's see," Ralphie thought out loud, "the storm has to rain out. Out. Down. Up . . . up with the updraft. . . . Freeze, fall, melt . . . melted snow falling . . . falling down. Down and out. That's it! I, Weatherman, will get us out of this."

Follow me. Grab a snowflake!

Liz steered the glider-bus as we all jumped off. We each grabbed our own snowflake to ride on — at least for a minute.
"Excuse me," said Arnold, "but my snowflake's melting."
"We're getting rained out!" yelled D.A.

Next thing we knew, we were raining right into Carlos's rain catcher. "My rain catcher worked!" yelled Carlos. "It's already rained one inch. Plus eight kids and one teacher."

The only question was, now that we were *rained* out, how were we going to *get* out? Luckily, Liz had just driven the bus into the parking lot.

How do we get out of here?

Ms. Frizzle gave the thumbs-up sign to Liz. Then Liz spilled us right out of the rain catcher. As we landed on the ground just outside our school door, we grew back to our normal size.

Safely back in our classroom, we discussed what we had learned on our field trip.

"Wind, water, and heat can make a huge storm," began Wanda.

"Those same ingredients can also make a beautiful sunny day," Ms. Frizzle added. "It's all in the mixing."

Ralphie had just one thing to add. "From now on, I'm going to leave the job of making weather up to . . ."

"Weatherwoman!" shouted Keesha.

"C'mon, Keesha," said Ralphie, "you can't be Weatherwoman any more than I can be Weatherman. The job is bigger than both of us."

TELEPHONE: Ring! Ring!

EDITOR: Magic School Bus here, Editor speaking.

KID CALLER: I'm studying up to be Weatherwoman. Want to test me?

EDITOR: OK. What is weather?

KC: Weather is what the air is like above us, way up to the highest clouds, as well as all around us. Ask me another one.

EDITOR: True or false? Most raindrops start out as ice or snow.

KC: True! And sometimes, in a thunderstorm, you even get hail, which is chunks of ice that hit the ground before they melt. Ask me one more.

EDITOR: OK. We talked about heat, water, and moving air combining to make weather. But we left out another important ingredient.

KC: Land! For example, mountains can push air up, making thunderstorms. And they can also keep rain away.

EDITOR: That's right. Weather isn't quite as simple as Weatherman made it out to be. It can get pretty complicated. Now tell me something. Are you really studying to be Weatherwoman?

KC: Of course not! There's no such thing as Weatherwoman. Nobody *makes* the weather!

EDITOR: Not even Weatherlizard?

Shikka-shikka-KABOOM!!!

How Far Is the Storm?
An Activity for Parents and Kids

If you're right at the center of a thunderstorm, you can see the lightning and hear the thunder at almost the same time. But if you're any distance away from the center, you see the lightning before you hear the thunder. That's because the speed of light is faster than the speed of sound. Light travels faster, so you see the lightning first.

You can tell how many miles away the center of a thunderstorm is by counting the seconds between the lightning and thunder and dividing by 5. (Use a watch or clock with a second hand.) If the time between the thunder and lightning is 10 seconds, the center of the storm is 2 miles away, because 10 divided by 5 is 2. If the time is 15 seconds, the storm is 3 miles away. The more seconds you count, the farther away the storm is.

If you count the seconds between the lightning and the thunder a few times, and each time you count more seconds, the center of the storm is moving away, and it may be clearing up soon. If you count fewer seconds each time, the center of the storm is moving toward you. If the thunder and lightning occur at the same time, the center of the storm is directly above you. Remember what Arnold told you about lightning, and stay inside!